OUR TOWN

Thornton Wilder

D1115328

TECHNICAL DIRECTOR Maxwell Krohn
EDITORIAL DIRECTOR Justin Kestler
MANAGING EDITOR Ben Florman

SERIES EDITORS Boomie Aglietti, Justin Kestler
PRODUCTION Christian Lorentzen, Camille Murphy

WRITERS Ross Douthat, Sasha Haines-Stiles
EDITORS Jesse Hawkes, Matt Blanchard

This edition published by Spark Publishing

Spark Publishing
A Division of SparkNotes LLC
120 Fifth Avenue, 8th Floor
New York, NY 10011

02 03 04 05 SN 9 8 7 6 5 4 3 2 1

Please send all comments and questions or report errors to
feedback@sparknotes.com.

Library of Congress information available upon request

Printed and bound in the United States

RRD-C

ISBN 1-58663-483-6

Introduction:
Stopping to Buy Sparknotes on a Snowy Evening

Whose words these are you *think* you know.
Your paper's due tomorrow, though;
We're glad to see you stopping here
To get some help before you go.

Lost your course? You'll find it here.
Face tests and essays without fear.
Between the words, good grades at stake:
Get great results throughout the year.

Once school bells caused your heart to quake
As teachers circled each mistake.
Use SparkNotes and no longer weep,
Ace every single test you take.

Yes, books are lovely, dark, and deep,
But only what you grasp you keep,
With hours to go before you sleep,
With hours to go before you sleep.

Contents

NOTE: This SparkNote refers to the Perennial Classics edition of *Our Town*. With the exception of page numbers, there are no major differences between the numerous editions of the text.

CONTEXT

THORNTON WILDER WAS BORN in Madison, Wisconsin, in 1897. He attended Oberlin College in Ohio and then transferred to Yale University, graduating in 1920. After spending a year in Rome, he took a job teaching French at a prep school in New Jersey and started writing on the side. Wilder published his first novel, *The Cabala*, in 1926, but his first real taste of fame came when he was awarded the Pulitzer Prize for *The Bridge of San Luis Rey* (1927). The royalties from this novel allowed him to quit his teaching job, and he began to write full-time. Wilder quickly became a literary celebrity, keeping company with the likes of Ernest Hemingway, F. Scott Fitzgerald, and Gertrude Stein.

In the ideologically charged climate of the 1930s, however, Wilder came under attack from critics who branded his work escapist fare that refused to confront the gloomy reality of the Depression. Hurt by this criticism and frustrated by the failure of his 1934 novel *Heaven's My Destination*, Wilder turned to playwriting. *Our Town*, his most celebrated dramatic effort, opened on Broadway in 1938 to rave reviews. Audiences sensed the universality of the themes presented in the play, which enabled virtually every theatergoer to participate in the action onstage and identify with the characters. *Our Town* eventually won Wilder his second Pulitzer Prize, and went on to become one of the most performed American plays of the twentieth century.

In many ways, *Our Town* is Wilder's response to his critics. Major works from other American writers of the time—notably Edgar Lee Masters's *Spoon River Anthology* and Sherwood Anderson's *Winesburg, Ohio*—exposed the buried secrets, hypocrisy, and oppression lurking beneath the surface of American small town life. In *Our Town*, however, Wilder presents a far more celebratory picture of a small town, the fictional hamlet of Grover's Corners, New Hampshire. Wilder does not deny the fact that the town suffers from social injustice and hypocrisy, and he does not intend to idealize Grover's Corners as a bastion of uncompromising brotherly love. On the contrary, Wilder makes a point to include in the play characters who criticize small town life, and Grover's Corners specifically. However, Wilder does not wish to denounce the community simply because it contains some strains of hypocrisy. Instead, he peers into Grover's Corners in order to find lessons about life in a world that contains both virtue and vice. He tenderly tracks the residents' day-to-day activities, their triumphs and their sorrows, their casual conversations and their formal traditions—not because he wants to praise New Hampshire, but because he wants to praise humanity. Perhaps a political message in itself, *Our Town* privileges the study of human life and its complexities over blatantly political works that point fingers, stereotype others, and otherwise divide people from one another.

Wilder's principal message in *Our Town*—that people should appreciate the details and interactions of everyday life while they live them—became critical at a time when political troubles were escalating in Europe. World War II was on the horizon when the play hit theaters in 1938. It was a time of tremendous international tension, and citizens across the globe suffered from fear and uncertainty. *Our Town* directed attention away from these negative aspects of life in the late 1930s and focused instead on the aspects of the human experience that make life precious. Wilder revealed his faith in the stability and constancy of life through his depiction and discussion of the small town of Grover's Corners, with its "marrying . . . living and . . . dying."

The 1920s and 1930s proved to be the heyday of Wilder's career. He enlisted as a soldier and served in Europe during World War II, and though he continued his literary career upon his return to the United States, his output decreased during the next two decades. A later effort to write a novel, *The Eighth Day* (1967), met with mixed reviews. Wilder died in December 1975 at his home in Connecticut.

Plot Overview

Oᴜʀ ᴛᴏᴡɴ is introduced and narrated by the Stage Manager, who welcomes the audience to the fictional town of Grover's Corners, New Hampshire, early on a May morning in 1901. In the opening scene, the stage is largely empty, except for some tables and chairs that represent the homes of the Gibbs and Webb families, the setting of most of the action in Act I. The set remains sparse throughout the rest of the play.

After the Stage Manager's introduction, the activities of a typical day begin. Howie Newsome, the milkman, and Joe Crowell, Jr., the paperboy, make their delivery rounds. Dr. Gibbs returns from delivering a set of twins at one of the homes in town. Mrs. Gibbs and Mrs. Webb make breakfast, send their children off to school, and meet in their gardens to gossip. The two women also discuss their modest ambitions, and Mrs. Gibbs reveals that she longs to visit Paris.

Throughout the play, the characters pantomime their activities and chores. When Howie makes his milk deliveries, for example, no horse appears onstage despite the fact that he frequently addresses his horse as "Bessie." Howie does not actually hold anything in his hands, but he pantomimes carrying bottles of milk, and the sound of clinking milk bottles comes from offstage. This deliberate abandonment of props goes hand in hand with the minimal set.

The Stage Manager interrupts the action. He calls Professor Willard and then Mr. Webb out onto the stage to tell the audience some basic facts about Grover's Corners. Mr. Webb not only reports to the audience, but also takes questions from some "audience members" who are actually characters in the play seated in the audience.

Afternoon arrives, school lets out, and George Gibbs meets his neighbor Emily Webb outside the gate of her house. We see the first inkling of George and Emily's romantic affection for one another during this scene and during Emily's subsequent conversation with her mother. The Stage Manager thanks and dismisses Emily and Mrs. Webb, then launches into a discussion of a time capsule that will be placed in the foundation of a new bank building in town. He tells us that he wishes to put a copy of *Our Town* into this time capsule.

Now evening, a choir in the orchestra pit begins to sing "Blessed Be the Tie That Binds." The choir, directed by the bitter yet comical choirmaster Simon Stimson, continues to sing as George and Emily talk to each other through their open windows. Mrs. Webb, Mrs. Gibbs, and their gossipy friend Mrs. Soames return home from choir practice and chat about the choirmaster's alcoholism. The women return to their respective homes. George and his sister Rebecca sit at a window and look outside. Rebecca ponders the position of Grover's Corners within the vastness of the universe, which she believes is contained within "the Mind of God." Night has fallen on Grover's Corners, and the first act comes to an end.

Act II takes place three years later, on George and Emily's wedding day. George tries to visit his fiancée, but he is shooed away by Mr. and Mrs. Webb, who insist that it is bad luck for the groom to see the bride-to-be on the wedding day anytime before the ceremony. Mrs. Webb goes upstairs to make sure Emily does not come downstairs. George is left alone with Mr. Webb. The young man and his future father-in-law awkwardly discuss marriage and how to be a virtuous husband.

The Stage Manager interjects and introduces a flashback to the previous year. George and Emily are on their way home from school. George has just been elected class president and Emily has just been elected secretary and treasurer. George has also become something of a local baseball star. Emily tells George that his popularity has made him "conceited and stuck-up." George, though hurt, thanks Emily for her honesty, but Emily becomes mortified by her own words and asks George to forget them. The two stop at Mr. Morgan's drugstore for ice-cream sodas and, over the course of their drink, admit their mutual affection. George decides to scrap his plan of attending agriculture school in favor of staying in Grover's Corners with Emily.

We return to the day of the wedding in 1904. Both the bride and groom feel jittery, but their parents calm them down and the ceremony goes ahead as planned. The Stage Manager acts as the clergyman. The newlyweds run out through the audience, and the second act ends with the Stage Manager's announcement that it is time for another intermission.

Act III takes place nine years later, in a cemetery on a hilltop overlooking the town. Emily has died in childbirth and is about to be buried. The funeral party occupies the back of the stage. The most prominent characters in this act, the dead souls who already inhabit the cemetery, sit in chairs at the front of the stage. Among the dead are Mrs. Gibbs, Mrs. Soames, Wally Webb, and Simon Stimson. As the funeral takes place, the dead speak, serving as detached witnesses. Death has rendered them largely indifferent to earthly events. Emily joins the dead, but she misses her previous life and decides to go back and relive part of it. The other souls disapprove and advise Emily to stay in the cemetery.

With the aid of the Stage Manager, Emily steps into the past, revisiting the morning of her twelfth birthday. Howie Newsome and Joe Crowell, Jr. make their deliveries as usual. Mrs. Webb gives her daughter some presents and calls to Mr. Webb. As Emily participates, she also watches the scene as an observer, noting her parents' youth and beauty. Emily now has a nostalgic appreciation for everyday life that her parents and the other living characters do not share. She becomes agonized by the beauty and transience of everyday life and demands to be taken back to the cemetery. As Emily settles in among the dead souls, George lays prostrate by her tomb. "They don't understand," she says of the living. The stars come out over Grover's Corners, and the play ends.

CHARACTER LIST

Stage Manager The host of the play and the dramatic equivalent of an omniscient narrator. The Stage Manager exercises control over the action of the play, cueing the other characters, interrupting their scenes with his own interjections, and informing the audience of events and objects that we cannot see. Although referred to only as Stage Manager and not by a name, he occasionally assumes other roles, such as an old woman, a druggist, and a minister. Interacting with both the world of the audience and the world of the play's characters, he occupies a godlike position of authority.

George Gibbs Dr. and Mrs. Gibbs's son. A decent, upstanding young man, George is a high school baseball star who plans to attend the State Agricultural School after high school. His courtship of Emily Webb and eventual marriage to her is central to the play's limited narrative action. Wilder uses George and Emily's relationship to ponder the questions of love and marriage in general.

Emily Webb Mr. and Mrs. Webb's daughter and Wally's older sister. Emily is George's schoolmate and next-door neighbor, then his fiancée, and later his wife. She is an excellent student and a conscientious daughter. After dying in childbirth, Emily joins the group of dead souls in the local cemetery and attempts to return to the world of the living. Her realization that human life is precious because it is fleeting is perhaps the central message of the play.

Dr. Gibbs George's father and the town doctor. Dr. Gibbs is also a Civil War expert. His delivery of twins just before the play opens establishes the themes of birth, life, and daily activity. He and his family are neighbors to the Webbs.

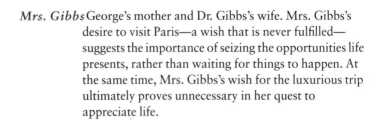

Mrs. Gibbs George's mother and Dr. Gibbs's wife. Mrs. Gibbs's desire to visit Paris—a wish that is never fulfilled—suggests the importance of seizing the opportunities life presents, rather than waiting for things to happen. At the same time, Mrs. Gibbs's wish for the luxurious trip ultimately proves unnecessary in her quest to appreciate life.

Mr. Webb Emily's father and the publisher and editor of the Grover's Corners Sentinel. Mr. Webb's report to the audience in Act I is both informative and interactive, as his question-and-answer session draws the audience physically into the action of the play.

Mrs. Webb Emily's mother and Mr. Webb's wife. At first a no-nonsense woman who does not cry on the morning of her daughter's marriage, Mrs. Webb later shows her innocent and caring nature, worrying during the wedding that she has not taught her daughter enough about marriage.

Mrs. Soames A gossipy woman who sings in the choir along with Mrs. Webb and Mrs. Gibbs. Mrs. Soames appears in the group of dead souls in Act III. One of the few townspeople we meet outside of the Webb and Gibbs families, Mrs. Soames offers a sense of the interrelated nature of the lives of the citizens of Grover's Corners.

Simon Stimson The choirmaster, whose alcoholism and undisclosed "troubles" have been the subject of gossip in Grover's Corners for quite some time. Wilder uses Mr. Stimson's misfortunes to explore the limitations of small town life. Mr. Stimson appears in the group of dead souls in Act III, having committed suicide by hanging himself in his attic. He is perhaps most notable for his short speech in Act III, when he says that human existence is nothing but "[i]gnorance and blindness."

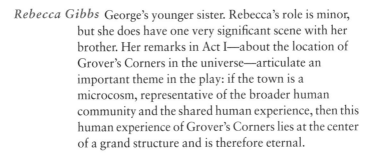

Rebecca Gibbs George's younger sister. Rebecca's role is minor, but she does have one very significant scene with her brother. Her remarks in Act I—about the location of Grover's Corners in the universe—articulate an important theme in the play: if the town is a microcosm, representative of the broader human community and the shared human experience, then this human experience of Grover's Corners lies at the center of a grand structure and is therefore eternal.

Wally Webb Emily's younger brother. Wally is a minor figure, but he turns up in Act III among the group of dead souls. Wally dies young, the result of a burst appendix on a Boy Scout trip. His untimely death underscores the brief and fleeting nature of life.

Howie Newsome The local milkman. Howie's reappearance during every morning scene—once each in Acts I, II, and III—highlights the continuity of life in Grover's Corners and in the general human experience.

Joe Crowell, Jr. The paperboy. Joe's routine of delivering papers to the same people each morning emphasizes the sameness of daily life in Grover's Corners. We see this sameness continue when Joe's younger brother, Si, takes over the route for him. Despite this sameness, however, each of the conversations Joe has while on his route is unique, suggesting that while his activities are monotonous, daily life is not.

Si Crowell Joe's younger brother, also a paperboy. Si's assumption of his brother's former job contributes to the sense of constancy that characterizes Grover's Corners throughout the play.

Professor Willard A professor at the State University who gives the audience a report on Grover's Corners. Professor Willard appears once and then disappears. His role in the play is to interact with the audience and to inform theatergoers of the specifics of life in Grover's Corners. His reference to Native Americans reflects

CHARACTER LIST

Wilder's understanding that the European ancestors of the current population in Grover's Corners replaced and extinguished the existing Native American populations.

Constable Warren A local policeman. Constable Warren keeps a watchful eye over the community. His personal knowledge of and favor with the town's citizens bespeaks the close-knit nature of the town.

Sam Craig Emily Webb's cousin, who has left Grover's Corners to travel west, but returns for her funeral in Act III. Though originally from the town, Sam has the air of an outsider. His unawareness of the events that have occurred in Grover's Corners during his absence parallels the audience's own unawareness.

Joe Stoddard The town undertaker. Joe prepares Emily's grave and remarks on how sad it is to bury young people. This statement emphasizes a theme that grows ever more apparent throughout the play and receives its most explicit discussion in Act III: the transience of human life.

Analysis of Major Characters

Stage Manager

An authoritative figure who resembles a narrator as he guides the audience through the play, the Stage Manager is an unconventional character in the canon of dramatic literature. He is not simply a character in the play. As his name suggests, he could be considered a member of the crew staging the play as well. He exists simultaneously in two dramatic realms. At the beginning of Act I, he identifies the play and the playwright, and introduces the director, the producer, and the actors. Furthermore, every act begins and ends with the Stage Manager's expositions and announcements. During each act, he frequently interrupts the play's action for the purpose of cueing another scene, providing the audience with pertinent information, or commenting on what has just happened or what is about to happen. All of these functions suggest that even though the Stage Manager occupies center stage, he is neither an actor nor a character, but rather someone who works behind the scenes.

But while the Stage Manager occupies a position outside of the narrative action—that is, outside of the play's central plot—he does occasionally assume the role of an inhabitant of Grover's Corners. For example, in Act II, after narrating the action, cueing a flashback, and changing the set to prepare for the next scene, he steps directly into the plot and becomes Mr. Morgan, the drugstore owner who serves ice-cream sodas to Emily Webb and George Gibbs. The Stage Manager is just as adept at changing sets as he is at changing roles, and this versatility enables him to exist both within the world of Grover's Corners and within the world that the audience occupies. Wilder deliberately makes the Stage Manager's location in the play ambiguous, because it is precisely this ambiguity that allows the Stage Manager to bridge the gap between the audience and the characters onstage.

The Stage Manager essentially plays the role of the audience's guide. He breaks through the fourth wall—the imaginary barrier between the audience and the action on the stage—to facilitate a dialogue between the audience and the content of the play. Indeed, through the Stage Manager, the interaction between the audience and the play actually becomes part of the content of the play itself. It is not clear whether the Stage Manager is a native of the town or an outsider who has been given a privileged view of Grover's Corners. This ambiguity makes him both familiar and mysterious and ultimately gives him a metaphorical role in the play, hinting at the presence of a God. Although Our Town avoids discussion of religion, Wilder hints that a spiritual force or entity manages human life in much the same way that the Stage Manager dictates the flow of this play, or as the stage manager of any play dictates its dramatic production. In any case, the Stage Manager makes great demands on the members of the audience to be active participants in the play. His presence blatantly disobeys the theatrical convention that has traditionally separated the audience from the events onstage.

EMILY WEBB

> Do *any human beings ever realize life while they
> live it?* — *every, every minute?*
>
> (See QUOTATIONS, p. 47)

With the exception of the Stage Manager, Emily is Our Town's most significant figure. Emily and George Gibbs's courtship becomes the basis of the text's limited narrative action—these two characters thus prove extremely significant not only to the play's events but also to its themes. In Act I, Emily displays her affection for George by agreeing to help him with his homework. In Act II, the play bears witness to Emily's marriage to George, and the young couple's wedding becomes emblematic of young love. In Act III, when the play's themes become fully apparent, Emily emerges as the primary articulator of these themes. After her death, Emily joins the dead souls in the town cemetery and begins to view earthly life and human beings from a new perspective. She realizes that the living "don't understand" the importance of human existence. After reliving her twelfth birthday, Emily sees that human beings fail to recognize the transience of life and to appreciate it while it lasts. This conclusion, which Emily expresses in her agonized wish to leave her birthday and return to the cemetery, encapsulates the play's most important theme: the transience of individual human lives in the face of general human and natural stability.

GEORGE GIBBS

Well, I think that's just as important as college is,
and even more so. That's what I think.

(See QUOTATIONS, p. 45)

If Emily displays an awareness—even if only after death—of the transience of human existence, George Gibbs lives his life in the dark. George is an archetypal all-American boy. A local baseball star and the president of his senior class in high school, he also possesses innocence and sensitivity. He is a good son, although like many children he sometimes neglects his chores. George expects to inherit his uncle's farm and plans to go to agriculture school; he ultimately scraps that plan, however, in favor of remaining in Grover's Corners to marry Emily. Indeed, all of George's achievements prove less important to him than Emily. She is George's closest neighbor since early childhood, and he declares his love for her in all-American fashion, over an ice-cream soda.

The revelation of Emily's death at the start of Act III draws attention to the thematic significance of George's life. The fact that George lays down prostrate at Emily's grave vividly illustrates Wilder's message that human beings do not fully appreciate life while they live it. The group of dead souls looks on George's prostrate body with confusion and disapproval, and Emily asks, rhetorically, "They don't understand, do they?" Instead of mourning for his lost wife, the dead suggest, George should be enjoying his life and the lives of those around him before he too dies. Wilder forces the audience to pity George, partly because of the tragedy he has suffered in Emily's death, but also because he epitomizes the human tragedy of caring too much about things that cannot change. At the same time, seeing George's pitiable condition, we realize that the dead souls' demand that George stifle his emotions is difficult, if not impossible. In this light, Wilder implies that perhaps the demanding dead souls "don't understand" either.

CHARACTER ANALYSIS

THEMES, MOTIFS & SYMBOLS

THEMES

Themes are the fundamental and often universal ideas explored in a literary work.

THE TRANSIENCE OF HUMAN LIFE

Although Wilder explores the stability of human traditions and the reassuring steadfastness of the natural environment, the individual human lives in *Our Town* are transient, influenced greatly by the rapid passage of time. The Stage Manager often notes that time seems to pass quickly for the people in the play. At one point, having not looked at his watch for a while, the Stage Manager misjudges the time, which demonstrates that sometimes even the timekeeper himself falls victim to the passage of time.

In light of the fact that humans are powerless to stem the advance of time, Wilder ponders whether human beings truly appreciate the precious nature of a transient life. Act I, which the Stage Manager entitles "Daily Life," testifies to the artfulness and value of routine daily activity. Simple acts such as eating breakfast and feeding chickens become subjects of dramatic scenes, indicating the significance Wilder sees in such seemingly mundane events. Wilder juxtaposes this flurry of everyday activity with the characters' inattentiveness to it. The characters are largely unaware of the details of their lives and tend to accept their circumstances passively. The Gibbs and Webb families rush through breakfast, and the children rush off to school, without much attention to one another. They, like most human beings, maintain the faulty assumption that they have an indefinite amount of time on Earth. Mrs. Gibbs refrains from insisting that her husband take her to Paris because she thinks there will always be time to convince him later.

The dead souls in Act III emphasize this theme of transience, disapproving of and chastising the living for their "ignorance" and "blindness." The dead even view George's grief and prostration upon Emily's grave as a pitiable waste of human time. Instead of grieving for the dead, they believe, the living should be enjoying the time they still have on Earth.

The medium of theater perfectly suits Wilder's intent to make ordinary lives and actions seem extraordinary, as the perspective of the dead souls parallels the audience's perspective. Just as the dead souls' distance finally enables them to appreciate the daily events in Grover's Corners, so too does the audience's outsider perspective render daily events valuable. We have never before witnessed a Gibbs family breakfast, and when the scene is dramatized on the stage, we see it as significant. Indeed, every action on the stage becomes significant, from Howie Newsome's milk delivery to the town choir practice.

The Importance of Companionship

Because birth and death seem inevitable, the most important stage of life is the middle one: the quest for companionship, friendship, and love. Humans have some degree of control over this aspect of life. Though they may not be fully aware of their doing so, the residents of Grover's Corners constantly take time out of their days to connect with each other, whether through idle chat with the milkman or small talk with a neighbor. The most prominent interpersonal relationship in the play is a romance—the courtship and marriage of George and Emily—and Wilder suggests that love epitomizes human creativity and achievement in the face of the inevitable advance of time.

Though romance is prominent in *Our Town*, it is merely the most vivid among a wide range of bonds that human beings are capable of forging. Wilder depicts a number of different types of relationships, and though some are merely platonic, all are significant. From the beginning of Act I, the Stage Manager seeks to establish a relationship with the audience, which forges a tie between the people onstage and the audience offstage. Within the action of the play, we witness the milkman and the paperboy chatting with members of the Gibbs and Webb families as they deliver their goods. The children walk to and from school in groups or pairs. Mrs. Gibbs and Mrs. Webb, next-door neighbors, meet in their yards to talk. We glimpse Mr. and Mrs. Webb and Dr. and Mrs. Gibbs in private conversation. As Mrs. Gibbs articulates, "Tain't natural to be lonesome."

Even the play's title—using the collective pronoun "[o]ur"—underscores the human desire for community. Many aspects of the play attest to the importance of community and companionship: the welcoming introduction from the Stage Manager; the audience participation, through the placement among the audience of actors within the audience who interact with those onstage; and the presence of numerous groups in the play, such as the choir, the wedding party, the funeral party, and the group of dead souls.

THE ARTIFICIALITY OF THE THEATER

Wilder does not pretend that his play represents a slice of real life. The events that occur onstage could easily be moments in real lives—a milkman delivers milk, a family has a hurried weekday breakfast, two young people fall in love—but Wilder undermines this appearance of reality by filling the play with devices that emphasize the artificiality of theater. The Stage Manager is the most obvious of these devices, functioning as a sort of narrator or modernized Greek chorus who comments on the play's action while simultaneously involving himself in it. The Stage Manager speaks directly to the audience and acknowledges our lack of familiarity with Grover's Corners and its inhabitants. He also manipulates the passage of time, incorporating flashbacks that take us—and the characters—back in time to relive certain significant moments. These intentional disruptions of the play's chronology prevent us from believing that what we see onstage could be real. Rather, the life we see on the stage becomes merely representative of real life, and is thus a fair target for Wilder's metaphorical and symbolic manipulation. Wilder's parallel positioning of the realm of the play and the real world implies a separation between the two. However, rather than distance the audience from the events on the stage, Wilder acknowledges the artificial nature of the stage and thus bridges the gap between the audience and the onstage events. This closeness between the audience and the story forces the audience to identify more fully with the characters and events.

MOTIFS

Motifs are recurring structures, contrasts, or literary devices that can help to develop and inform the text's major themes.

THE STAGES OF LIFE

The division of the play's narrative action into three acts reflects Wilder's division of human life into three parts: birth, love and marriage, and death. The play opens at the dawn of a new day with a literal birth: at the very beginning of Act I, we learn that Dr. Gibbs has just delivered twins. Act II details George and Emily's courtship and marriage. Act III features a funeral and delves into the possibilities of an afterlife. The overall arc of the story carries the audience from the beginning of life to its end. Our observation of the lives of the Gibbs and Webb families, condensed into a few short hours, leads us to realize that the human experience, while multifaceted, is nevertheless brief and precious. Indeed, Wilder demonstrates how quickly the characters proceed from stage to stage. George and Emily marry in Act II, but they appear just as nervous and childish as they do in Act I. The second stage of life has snuck up on them. This intermingling of the stages of life recurs later, when the second stage of Emily's life, her marriage, is suddenly cut short when she dies in childbirth.

NATURAL CYCLES

While *Our Town* spans the course of many years, from 1899 through 1913, it also collapses its events into the span of one day. It opens with a morning scene and ends with a nighttime scene: Act I begins just before dawn, and Act III ends at 11 P.M. The play also metaphorically spans the course of a human life, tracing the path from birth in Dr. Gibbs's delivery of twins in the opening scene, to death in Emily's funeral in the final scene. The span of a life parallels the span of the day: birth is related to dawn, and death is related to night. Wilder's attention to natural cycles highlights his themes of the transience of life and the power of time. While a single human life comprises only one finite revolution from birth to death, the world continues to spin, mothers continue to give birth, and human beings continue to exist as just one part of the universe.

MORNING

Morning scenes are prominent in each of the play's three acts: Act I depicts the ordinary morning activities of the townspeople, Act II portrays the Gibbs and Webb families on the morning of Emily and George's wedding, and Act III includes Emily's return to the morning of her twelfth birthday. Despite differences in context and circumstance, each morning scene appears strikingly similar to the others, which emphasizes the lack of change in Grover's Corners. In each of the three scenes, Howie Newsome delivers milk and a Crowell boy delivers newspapers. Yet while stability is clearly a feature of life in the town, Wilder shows that it often leads to indifference. Because each day appears more or less the same as the previous one, the townspeople fail to observe or appreciate the subtle, life-affirming peculiarities each day brings.

Wilder treats each of the three mornings differently, which highlights the subtle differences between them. He presents the first morning as merely an average day, but as foreign observers, we appreciate the novelty of the experience. On the morning of the wedding, Wilder shows how impending events disturb the morning rituals and create a unique experience. Lastly, Wilder presents the morning of Emily's twelfth birthday through the eyes of her dead soul, a perspective that gives the morning a truly extraordinary and beautiful transience. Wilder implies that though mundane routines and events may generally be repetitive, the details are what make life interesting and deserve attention.

THE MANIPULATION OF TIME

Events do not progress chronologically in *Our Town*. The Stage Manager has the ability to cue scenes whenever he wishes, and can call up previous moments in the lives of the characters at will. The most prominent of these manipulations of time are the flashbacks to Mr. Morgan's soda fountain and to Emily's twelfth birthday. Wilder explicitly shuffles the flow of time within the play to engage, please, and inform his audience in three ways. First, Wilder uses the lack of chronological order to engage his audience by overturning their expectations of the theater. As opposed to showing us the progression of a day, or of a life, Wilder shows us disparate moments, reordering them in a way that best reflects his—and the Stage Manager's—philosophical themes. Second, the Stage Manager's informal treatment of the flow of time adds to the play's pleasing conversational tone. The Stage Manager's desire to flash back to George and Emily's first date at the drugstore makes him seem just as curious about the origins of the couple's relationship as we are. Third, by including flashbacks within a linear narrative, Wilder reminds the audience how swiftly time passes. The characters spend precious time flashing back in their own minds, appreciating past moments in retrospect rather than recognizing the value of moments as they occur in the present.

SYMBOLS

Symbols are objects, characters, figures, or colors used to represent abstract ideas or concepts.

THE TIME CAPSULE

In Act I, the Stage Manager briefly mentions a time capsule that is being buried in the foundation of a new building in town. The citizens of Grover's Corners wish to include the works of Shakespeare, the Constitution, and the Bible; the Stage Manager says he would like to throw a copy of *Our Town* into the time capsule as well. The time capsule embodies the human desire to keep a record of the past. Accordingly, it also symbolizes the idea that certain parts of the past deserve to be remembered over and above others. Wilder wishes to challenge this latter notion. He has the Stage Manager place *Our Town* into the capsule so the people opening it in the future will not only appreciate the daily lives of the townspeople from the past, but also their own daily lives in the future.

The self-referential notion of placing the play into the time capsule also carries symbolic weight. The fact that *Our Town* is actually mentioned within *Our Town* clearly shows Wilder's intent to break down the wall that divides the world of the play from the world of the audience. By mentioning his own play within his play, Wilder acknowledges that his text is artificial, a literary creation. Even more important, however, the Stage Manager's wish to put the play into the capsule lends historic significance to the audience's watching of *Our Town*. He implies that even the current production of the play—its sets, lights, actors, and audience—is in itself an important detail of life.

HOWIE NEWSOME AND THE CROWELL BOYS

Each of the three morning scenes in *Our Town* features the milkman, Howie Newsome, and a paperboy—either Joe or Si Crowell. Throughout the play, the Stage Manager and other characters, such as Mr. Webb in his report in Act I, discuss the stability of Grover's Corners—nothing changes much in the town. Howie and the Crowell boys illustrate this constancy of small town life. They appear in 1901, just as they do in 1904 and in the flashback to 1899. Because Grover's Corners is Wilder's microcosm of human life in general, Howie and the Crowells represent not only the stability of life in Grover's Corners, but the stability of human life in general. The milkman and the paperboys embody the persistence of human life and the continuity of the human experience from year to year, from generation to generation. Moreover, the fact that Si replaces his brother Joe shows that the transience of individual lives actually becomes a stabilizing force. Growing from birth toward death, humans show how the finite changes in individual lives are simply part of stable cycles.

The Hymn "Blessed Be the Tie That Binds"

A choir sings the hymn "Blessed Be the Tie That Binds" in the background three different times throughout the play. In part, the repetition of the song emphasizes Wilder's general notion of stability and tradition. However, the Christian hymn primarily embodies Wilder's belief that the love between human beings is divine in nature. The "tie" in the song's lyrics refers to both the tie between humans and God and the ties among humans themselves.

The three scenes that include the hymn also prominently feature Emily and George, highlighting the "tie that binds" the two of them. The first instance of the song comes during a choir practice, which occurs simultaneously with George and Emily's conversation through their open windows in Act I. The second instance comes during the wedding ceremony in Act II. The third instance comes during Emily's funeral, as her body is interred and she joins the dead in the cemetery, leaving George behind. By associating this particular song with the play's critical moments, Wilder foregrounds the notion of companionship as an essential, even divine, feature of human life. The hymn may add some degree of Christian symbolism to the play, but Wilder, for the most part, downplays any discussion of specifically Christian symbols. He concentrates on the hymn not because of its allusion to the fellowship between Christians in particular, but rather because of what it says about human beings in general.

SYMBOLS

Summary & Analysis

Act I: Part one

PART ONE: *From the beginning of the Act through Mrs. Gibbs and Mrs. Webb's conversation in the garden*

SUMMARY

The play opens with a view of an empty, curtainless, half-lighted stage. The Stage Manager enters and arranges minimal scenery—a table and three chairs—to represent two houses, one on each side of the stage. The houselights dim as the Stage Manager moves about the stage. When the theater is completely dark, he introduces the play, naming the playwright, producers, director, and cast. He then identifies the setting: the town of Grover's Corners, New Hampshire, just before dawn on May 7, 1901.

The Stage Manager speaks directly to the audience as he maps out local landmarks. The audience must use its imagination, since the minimalist set does not detail any of these landmarks, which include Main Street, the public schools, Town Hall, and several churches. The Stage Manager explains that the two sets of tables and chairs denote the homes of the Gibbs family and the Webb family. As he speaks, his assistants wheel out two trellises to represent the back doors of Mrs. Webb's and Mrs. Gibbs's homes. "There's some scenery for those who think they have to have scenery," the Stage Manager comments. He mentions that the 5:45 A.M. train to Boston is just about to depart. A train whistle blows offstage and the Stage Manager looks at his watch, nodding.

As dawn breaks over Grover's Corners, the Stage Manager proceeds to introduce the audience to the town's inhabitants. We witness the beginning of a new day in the Webb and Gibbs households and observe the morning activities of the two families and a few other townspeople. The characters pantomime many of their actions due to the absence of props and scenery. Mrs. Webb and Mrs. Gibbs enter their respective kitchens, light their stoves, and begin making breakfast. The Stage Manager informs the audience that both Dr. Gibbs and Mrs. Gibbs have died since 1901, when this scene originally took place.

Dr. Gibbs, on his way home from delivering a local woman's twin babies, stops to chat briefly with the paperboy, Joe Crowell, Jr. They discuss the upcoming marriage of a local schoolteacher. Dr. Gibbs stands in the street and reads the paper as Joe exits. The Stage Manager interrupts the immediate action to inform the audience that Joe would go on the become the brightest boy in high school and study at Massachusetts Tech. Well on his way to becoming a successful engineer, Joe would be killed in France during World War I.

Howie Newsome, the milkman, enters with an invisible horse. Howie stops to converse with Dr. Gibbs, who gives him the news of the twins' birth. After Howie delivers his milk to the Gibbs residence, Dr. Gibbs goes inside and greets his wife, who has made coffee for him. Mrs. Gibbs asks her husband to speak to their teenage son, George, about helping around the house more often. Next door, Mrs. Webb calls her children—Emily and Wally—down to breakfast. In the Gibbs household, George and his sister, Rebecca, enter the kitchen and sit at the table. Both pairs of children chatter over breakfast, then go outside, meet in the street, and hurry off to school together.

Left alone, Mrs. Gibbs and Mrs. Webb go outside into their gardens. The two women see each other and come together for a chat. Mrs. Gibbs tells Mrs. Webb that she has some news: a traveling secondhand furniture salesman recently offered her the hefty sum of $350 for her highboy, an old piece of furniture. The women discuss whether Mrs. Gibbs should accept the offer and what she would do with the money. Mrs. Gibbs says that if she does decide to sell the highboy, she hopes to live out the "dream of [her] life" and travel to Paris for a visit. Her excitement is tempered, however, by the fact that Dr. Gibbs has already told her that "traipsin' about Europe" might make him disheartened with Grover's Corners, and thus thinks a trip to Paris might be a bad idea. Mrs. Gibbs says that her husband only cares about going to Civil War battlefields. Mrs. Webb remarks that her husband, an eager student of Napoleonic history, greatly admires Dr. Gibbs's Civil War expertise. At this point, the Stage Manager interrupts abruptly and tips his hat to the two women, who nod in recognition. He thanks the two ladies, and they return to their houses and disappear from the stage.

ANALYSIS

As its title suggests, *Our Town* is a play about a typical town—in this case, a typical American town. The Stage Manager tells us that we are peering in on Grover's Corners, New Hampshire, but we get the feeling that we could be in any small American town. The introduction—wherein the Stage Manager acquaints us with the town's layout, its people, and their activities—establishes a familiarity between the world onstage and the world offstage. The Stage Manager speaks directly to the audience, as if the audience members are people passing through the town, rather than distant, detached theatergoers.

The action in this section does not revolve around a dramatic incident, but rather serves to establish a sense of the town's atmosphere and the temperament of its people. Moreover, Wilder's presentation of the morning rituals of two families and the activities of the town gives us insight into what the townspeople's lives look like not just on this morning, but perhaps on every morning. The Stage Manager correctly notes that the train whistle will blow around 5:45 A.M., looking at his watch and nodding to emphasize the predictability and regularity of the town's activities. Wilder discusses the importance of these daily activities throughout the remainder of the play.

The Gibbses and the Webbs represent two archetypal American families, just as Grover's Corners represents the archetypal small American town. The two families' homes are the only homes into which we are allowed to see, and their ambitions and lives are the only ones to which we are given extended access. We see other characters, such as Howie Newsome and Joe Crowell, Jr., only as transient figures projected against the lives of the Gibbses and Webbs.

Wilder establishes the centrality of these particular families in the opening scenes, but he does so while focusing on what could be the daily activities and aspirations of any middle-class American family. Dr. Gibbs and the paperboy gossip about the marriage of a local schoolteacher, the children converse about schoolwork and their allowances, and Mrs. Gibbs talks about her lifelong desire to take a vacation in Europe. Neither poor nor rich, the Gibbses and Webbs live modest, but busy and full lives.

Wilder chooses to portray two families so that he can emphasize their similarities. Both homes have the same layout and the same number of chairs at the table. Both Mrs. Webb and Mrs. Gibbs work in their respective gardens, just as both Mr. Webb, as the editor of the local newspaper, and Dr. Gibbs, as the town doctor, occupy positions of social status. Moreover, both men have the similar hobby of the study of wars. Though these two families are archetypically American, *Our Town* illustrates the universality of human concerns and desires, regardless of national identity.

The play focuses on characters rather than on dramatic action in order to protect this sense of universal applicability. No profound conflicts emerge that lead us to believe that life in Grover's Corners differs from life anywhere else. Wilder wants us to sympathize with his characters and to put ourselves in their shoes, not to view them as people with dramatic problems foreign to our own. We are drawn in by the modest but ardent hopes of people such as Mrs. Gibbs, who yearns for a vacation, and the satisfactions of those such as her husband, who has just successfully delivered twins. Wilder emphasizes these sorts of everyday ambitions and accomplishments throughout the play. The hopes, dreams, and morning rituals of the townspeople we meet are characteristic of people all the world over. Likewise, the townspeople's personal tragedies echo broader modern tragedies, evident when we learn that the prize pupil Joe Crowell, Jr. will meet an untimely end in World War I.

While most readers identify with the content of the play simply through the dialogue, Wilder augments the play's universality through the use of numerous theatrical techniques when the play is actually performed. The minimal scenery and pantomimed actions—the paperboy throws imaginary newspapers, the children pretend to eat breakfast—force each person in the audience to imagine objects that do not really exist. The imaginary quality of these objects makes the play more universal, since we, as members of the audience, can use our own sense of imagination to envision the props in our own way. This flexibility engages the audience and personalizes *Our Town* for each viewer, making the play more immediate and accessible.

Wilder further connects his play with the audience through the figure of the Stage Manager, whose bodily presence alone breaks the boundary separating the audience from the actors. The Stage Manager, whose very title reflects his intermediary function in the play, facilitates the viewer's communion with the action and characters. He alternately functions as a narrator communicating with the audience and as an inhabitant of Grover's Corners—he plays the role of Mr. Morgan in Act II, and other roles later. The Stage Manager, then, exists both inside and outside the world of the play, and he has the ability to draw the audience into the play person-ally. Moreover, as he does in the second half of Act I, he can engage the members of the town, drawing them out onto the stage to speak with the audience.

The play's very title contributes to this intimacy between the play and the audience. The Stage Manager frequently refers to the setting as "our town" rather than Grover's Corners, especially in the intro-duction. By announcing the play's author, director, producers, and so on, and by abruptly breaking in on the action to move the play along, the Stage Manager destroys the illusion that the play depicts real life. Instead, the play depicts a representative form of reality. We in the audience need not worry about suspending our disbelief because the Stage Manager allows us to accept the imaginary nature of the play. We identify with the characters in the play, but we iden-tify even more with the Stage Manager. Owing to the Stage Man-ager's presence, a person watching a performance of *Our Town* is likely to realize that the scenes onstage could be enacted anywhere, at any time.

ACT I: PART TWO

PART TWO: *From the introduction of Professor Willard to the end of the Act*

SUMMARY

> *So—people a thousand years from now.... This is the way we were: in our growing up and in our marrying and in our living and in our dying.*
>
> (See QUOTATIONS, p. 43)

After shooing Mrs. Webb and Mrs. Gibbs offstage, the Stage Man-ager announces that "we're going to skip a few hours," but first introduces an expert on Grover's Corners to give a "scientific account" of the town. Professor Willard, an academic from the State University, lays out a series of basic facts about Grover's Cor-ners—geological data, the ethnic makeup of the inhabitants, and population figures. Professor Willard mentions that the town is very homogeneous: nearly all the residents are white—primarily "English brachiocephalic blue-eyed stock"—and are overwhelm-ingly Republican and Protestant. The population is nearly constant, as the birth and death rates roughly balance each other. The Stage

Manager thanks and dismisses Professor Willard, then calls on Mr. Webb, the editor of the local paper, to give a "political and social report." Mrs. Webb comes onstage to announce that her husband has been delayed because he has just cut his hand while slicing an apple. Mr. Webb soon appears and gives his report, his finger bandaged in a handkerchief.

After Mr. Webb finishes his report, the Stage Manager asks if anyone in the audience has any questions for Mr. Webb. There are indeed several questions, shouted out by actors planted in the crowd. When a Woman in the Balcony asks how much drinking goes on in Grover's Corners, Mr. Webb replies that only a minimal amount takes place. A Belligerent Man demands to know whether the inhabitants of Grover's Corners are aware of "social injustice and industrial inequality" and whether any of them intends to do anything to solve these problems. Mr. Webb replies that while people in Grover's Corners talk about economic disparities all the time and want all "diligent" and "sensible" people to live well, the only thing they can do is try to help those who need help and leave other people alone. When a Lady in a Box asks if there is any "culture or love of beauty" in the town, Mr. Webb answers that though the town itself has little cosmopolitan culture, the residents appreciate the simple pleasures in life, such as the observation of nature. Done taking questions, Mr. Webb retires to his house and begins mowing the lawn. The Stage Manager announces that it is now early afternoon in Grover's Corners, but then notices that he has misjudged the time and that it is actually later in the afternoon than he thought.

Emily Webb enters, on her way home from school. She reaches her yard, jokes a little with her father, and picks some flowers. George Gibbs walks down Main Street, also coming home from school. He stops to say hello to Emily and compliments her on a speech she gave in class that day. The two talk about mathematics and Emily promises to help George with his homework. George starts to discuss his plans to become a farmer and eventually take over his Uncle Luke's farm, but he stops when Mrs. Webb comes outside. George says hello to Mrs. Webb, but then hastily leaves to go to the baseball field. Left alone with her mother, Emily asks if she is good-looking. Mrs. Webb scolds Emily for asking such a silly question, but assures her that she is pretty enough.

The Stage Manager interrupts again, thanking Emily and her mother, who withdraw from the stage. The Stage Manager announces that he has yet to reveal everything about Grover's Corners, and tells the audience about a time capsule being placed in the foundation of the new bank under construction in town. The prospective contents of the time capsule include issues of the New York Times and Mr. Webb's Sentinel, as well as a Bible, a copy of the Constitution, and a book of plays by William Shakespeare. The Stage Manager says that he will have a copy of this play, *Our Town*, placed in the cornerstone so that people in the future will know some simple facts about everyday life at the beginning of the twentieth century.

The lights dim as the Stage Manager speaks, and he announces that evening has fallen. A chorus in the orchestra pit, directed by Simon Stimson, begins singing the hymn "Blessed Be the Tie That Binds." George and Emily reappear onstage, sitting in their respective bedrooms and talking to each other through their open windows. The stage directions indicate that the two youngsters actually sit on the tops of two ladders. Dr. Gibbs calls to his son, asking him to come downstairs for a moment. When George descends, his father asks him to be more responsible around the house and to help his mother with chores more often. Ashamed, George begins to cry, and his father offers him a handkerchief. Before sending George back upstairs, Dr. Gibbs says that he will increase George's allowance because George will have more expenses as he grows older.

Meanwhile, the ladies—Mrs. Gibbs, Mrs. Webb, and Mrs. Soames— return home from choir practice. A tireless gossip, Mrs. Soames tries to strike up a conversation about the apparent alcoholism of the choirmaster, Mr. Stimson. Thinking the subject is inappropriate, Mrs. Gibbs and Mrs. Webb halt the discussion and say good night. Mrs. Gibbs goes inside and talks to her husband— about Mr. Stimson, no less—while Rebecca joins George at his upstairs window. The two youngsters stare out at the moon.

Mr. Webb comes home from his office at the newspaper. On his way, he encounters Constable Warren and the somewhat unsteady Mr. Stimson. Once home, Mr. Webb says good night to Emily, who is still awake and at her window, while across the way Rebecca and George continue to chat and look at the sky. Rebecca mentions a letter that her friend Jane once received. Rebecca recalls that the letter was addressed to "Jane Crofut; The Crofut Farm; Grover's Corners; Sutton County; New Hampshire; United States of America; Continent of North America; Western Hemisphere; the Earth; the Solar System; the Universe; the Mind of God." The Stage Manager reappears and announces the end of Act I, telling the audience they may now have a smoke if they wish.

ANALYSIS

Professor Willard's and Mr. Webb's direct addresses to the audience serve several purposes. First, the fact that the two men appear at the request of the Stage Manager establishes the Stage Manager as an almost godlike authority within the text of the play. He appears to manage everything that happens on the stage, halting the action at will, pulling characters away from their daily activities to converse with the audience, and asking them to leave the stage when their presence is no longer required. Second, Professor Willard's and Mr. Webb's reports, as well as Mr. Webb's question-and-answer session, strengthen the bond between the characters and the audience. The apparently spontaneous—though actually staged—interaction between the audience and Mr. Webb indicates Wilder's desire for the audience to feel included in the daily life of Grover's Corners. Third, the presentation of facts about the town's past and present complements the Stage Manager's own omniscient knowledge of the town's events and his foresight of the characters' deaths. Wilder implies that an accurate understanding of the town comes not only from meeting its current inhabitants but also from knowing its history. Finally, the two reports underscore how remarkably ordinary the town is, and how racially, ethnically, religiously, and politically homogenous. Professor Willard's geological references imply that very little has changed throughout the history of Grover's Corners, and his mention of the stagnant birth and death rates and lack of population change suggests that little change is expected in the future.

Though the character of the town as a whole changes little over the years, individual lives are transient. In the first half of Act I, the Stage Manager reflects upon the fact that Dr. and Mrs. Gibbs and Joe Crowell, Jr. have already died by the time *Our Town* is performed. In the second half of Act I, time passes quickly and even the Stage Manager mistakes the time, believing it is early afternoon but then realizing it must be later, since he can hear the children on their way home from school. Additionally, the Stage Manager foreshadows the fact that the play deals with both marriage and death before the evening ends when he says that the play details the "marrying . . . living and . . . dying" of the inhabitants of Grover's Corners. Moreover, Wilder foreshadows Emily and George's burgeoning romance through their uneasy conversations and through Dr. Gibbs's comment that George will soon need a larger allowance to take care of unspecified "things" associated with growing older. Wilder foreshadows Emily's death by describing her as an exemplary scholar with great potential—just like Joe Crowell, Jr., the prized student and engineer who had great potential but was tragically killed in World War I.

A number of scholars and reviewers have criticized the homogeneity of Grover's Corners, a largely white, Protestant town. *Our Town* has been derided as an escapist fantasy that ignores the realities of the racism, sexism, and economic hardship that defined American life during Wilder's era and that continue, to some degree, to define American life today. Some of these criticisms may be somewhat merited. *Our Town* does not offer a serious critique of social injustice, which makes the play appear out of step with and irrelevant to its own time. Nor does the play highlight the growing diversity in America at the time. While the Stage Manager mentions the presence of some Polish and Canuck, or French-Canadian, families in his opening remarks in Act I, these families do not appear in the play, and we do not hear of their experiences.

At the same time, Wilder appears to anticipate, and perhaps even encourage, such criticism even within the play itself. While the play may fail to address pressing social issues, it does not idealize the town and its citizens. The Belligerent Man who questions Mr. Webb attacks the townspeople's apparent lack of social activism, in effect stealing the thunder from Wilder's own critics. Similarly, Professor Willard provides a dark image of European influences upon Native American populations: "Yes . . . anthropological data: Early Amerindian stock. Cotahatchee tribes . . . no evidence before the tenth century of this era . . . now entirely disappeared. . . ." Details such as these indicate Wilder's intent to portray a community complete both with virtues and flaws.

Despite the townspeople's well-meaning nature, they have only a limited ability or willingness to act or confront societal problems. Mr. Webb and Constable Warren simply watch Mr. Stimson walk by in a drunken haze. Mr. Webb offers to walk with Mr. Stimson, but does not press the matter beyond the realm of polite interaction. Likewise, when Mrs. Gibbs mentions Stimson's drinking to Dr. Gibbs, he merely replies that "some people ain't made for small-town life." Dr. Gibbs feels more comfortable relegating problems such as alcoholism to other spheres of life, like the city. There is a sense that, though isolated, Grover's Corners is inextricably bound to the rest of the world and its accompanying problems. The residents of *Our Town* clearly have faults, but we recognize these faults as our own and take them to heart.

Wilder addresses the question of *Our Town*'s cultural relevance in the Stage Manager's discussion of the time capsule. In addition to the essential cultural and political artifacts that are deposited in the time capsule—the Bible, the works of Shakespeare, the Constitution—the Stage Manager wishes to include this very play. The purpose of a time capsule is to give people in the future an accurate idea of what it was like to live in a previous time. A grandiose drama like Hamlet may be a pinnacle of human civilization's literary achievements, but it has an exceptional story, not one that details ordinary lives. *Our Town*, on the other hand, concerns an unexceptional group of people in an unexceptional town, and as such represents everyday life better than any of Shakespeare's writings. However, while concerned with ordinary events, *Our Town* will serve an extraordinary purpose: when the capsule is opened, it will show "people a thousand years from now . . . the way we were: in our growing up and in our marrying and in our living and in our dying." Wilder intends for his play not only to engage but also to inform its audiences. In depicting ordinary life in a small town, the play becomes relevant to the human desire to know the details of human history.

ACT II

SUMMARY

> [P]eople are meant to go through life two by two.
> 'Tain't natural to be lonesome.
>
> (See QUOTATIONS, p. 44)

The Stage Manager watches the audience return from intermission, and announces that three years have passed. It is now July 7, 1904, just after commencement at the local high school. The Stage Manager tells us that the first act was called "Daily Life," and that this second act is entitled "Love and Marriage." He says that a third act will follow, and that the audience can guess what that act will be about.

We witness another morning scene, much like the first, except this time it is raining heavily. Howie Newsome delivers milk and runs into the paperboy—now Si Crowell, the younger brother of Joe Crowell, Jr.—and Constable Warren. They discuss the impending marriage of George Gibbs. Si bemoans the fact that George will have to stop playing baseball. He says George was the "best baseball pitcher Grover's Corners ever had." The Constable and Si continue on their way, and Howie stops to chat at the Gibbs household, where Mrs. Gibbs is preparing for the wedding guests she expects to host later that day. Howie then crosses the yard and talks to Mrs. Webb. Their conversation reveals to the audience that George has become engaged to Emily Webb.

Back in the Gibbs's kitchen, Dr. and Mrs. Gibbs reminisce about the morning of their own wedding. George comes downstairs and announces that he is going next door to see Emily. Mrs. Gibbs makes him put on overshoes because of the rain. George hurries across the yard, but Mrs. Webb will not let him see Emily because she believes it is bad luck for the groom to see the bride anytime on the wedding day prior to the ceremony. Mr. Webb agrees with this superstition, and Mrs. Webb runs upstairs to make sure Emily does not come down. Left alone, Mr. Webb and George awkwardly discuss weddings and the idea of what makes a happy marriage. The Webbs then shoo George out of the house.

The Stage Manager reappears and interrupts the action again. He announces that, before proceeding, we need to find out how George and Emily's relationship began. We flash back to the beginning of George and Emily's courtship, at the end of their junior year in high school. George and Emily appear onstage. George has just been elected president of his class, and Emily has been elected secretary and treasurer. Emily carries a handful of invisible books, which George offers to carry for her. As they walk home together, Emily remarks that a change has come over George since he became a local baseball star. She says he has become "conceited and stuck-up." Although hurt, George takes her words to heart. Emily, suddenly mortified at her own bluntness, apologizes to George and begins to cry.

George tells Emily not to be concerned and invites her to have an ice-cream soda with him at the local drugstore. The Stage Manager dons spectacles and assumes the role of the druggist, Mr. Morgan. Emily and George sit at the counter and talk about the future. George talks about his tentative plans to go to the State Agriculture

School. Throughout the conversation, however, George weighs the idea of continuing his formal education against the idea of staying in Grover's Corners with Emily, revealing his fondness for her.

The Stage Manager takes off his spectacles and returns us to the day of the wedding. He waits and watches while stagehands clear away the chairs and tables and set up rows of pews at center stage. After announcing that he will now play the role of the clergyman and that the play is about to get "pretty serious," the Stage Manager launches into a short sermon about the divine power that wills the existence of marriage and procreation and about the importance of marriage in human history.

The congregation streams in and fills the pews. Mrs. Webb enters last, and before she sits down, she turns toward the audience and talks for a moment about how girls lack adequate preparation for marriage. George makes his way from the back of the theater through the audience and toward the altar onstage. A group of George's baseball teammates heckle him good-naturedly, and the Stage Manager orders them offstage. At the front of the church, George withdraws nervously. When his mother leaves her seat and advances, he anxiously tells her that he does not want to grow up and get married. After George finally comes to his senses, Mrs. Gibbs fixes his tie. Emily, also feeling jittery, enters in her wedding dress and confesses her own apprehensions to her father. A choir has begun singing "Blessed Be the Tie That Binds." Mr. Webb tries to calm his daughter and then calls George over. Putting his arm around the couple, Mr. Webb tells George he is content to give away his daughter. His encouragement solaces George and Emily, who proceed with the wedding.

The Stage Manager begins the service, but Mrs. Soames drowns out his words while chattering noisily about how "lovely" she finds the wedding. After George and Emily exchange rings and a kiss, the scene freezes briefly in a tableau, and the Stage Manager, still acting as the clergyman, muses about the number of couples he has married over time. Without cynicism, he remarks that one in a thousand wedding ceremonies is interesting. The scene comes back to life as an organ plays the "Wedding March," and George and Emily run to the audience and down the aisle. The Stage Manager announces the end of Act II and a ten-minute intermission.

ANALYSIS

The similarity between the morning activities in Act I and Act II implies that an underlying stability defines life in Grover's Corners, despite the onset of marriage and other indications of individual growth and maturation. Though the Stage Manager says that several years have passed since Act I, very little in the town seems to have changed. Howie Newsome still delivers milk, a member of the Crowell family still delivers the papers, and the train whistle stills blows at 5:45 every morning. The Stage Manager's description of the passing of time emphasizes the difference between individual change and broader change. On an individual level, "babies that weren't even born before have begun talking regular sentences already; and a number of people who thought they were right young and spry have noticed that they can't bound up a flight of stairs like they used to." On a more general level, the Stage Manager notes the slow shifts in geology, saying that weather and erosion have gradually worn the mountains. Even though, as he says, "millions of gallons of water went by the mill" and the "sun's come up over a thousand times," these natural and environmental forces remain cyclical and steadfast.

Despite the fact that flashbacks typically heighten the sense that individual human lives pass quickly, the Stage Manager uses flashbacks to contribute to the sense of general stability. Here, he uses the technique of flashback to slow down time. He interrupts George and Emily's wedding day and returns to the moment at which their romantic relationship begins. In this case, the flashback offers a comparison between the two scenes that emphasizes the play's focus on stability. Emily and George's nervousness at the drugstore counter mirrors their wedding day jitters. Although the idea of a wedding suggests that the two young people should have matured, Emily and George remain childlike in their anxiousness. Comforting their children, the parents demonstrate the constancy of the dynamic between parent and child. This relation of thematically similar but temporally separated scenes implies that past, present, and future all bear a striking resemblance to each other.

The relationship between George and Emily comprises the central narrative of the play. Wilder traces the progression of George and Emily's love from initial neighborly friendliness to later romantic affection and marriage, and ultimately to grief over the loss of a loved one. With its rather generic emotions and rituals, Emily and George's relationship is representative of a broad spectrum of relationships in the play—including those of Dr. and Mrs. Gibbs and Mr. and Mrs. Webb—but it is the only relationship we see in its entirety, from start to finish. Wilder foregrounds George and Emily, suggesting that the couple's experience, with love as a central component, epitomizes the human experience. This focus on their relationship emphasizes one of the play's central themes, the human need for interaction and companionship. Throughout the course of the play we listen in on conversations among brothers and sisters, schoolmates, adults and children, choir members, and neighbors. Romantic love represents the most powerful version of this desire for companionship, for communion with another human being.

Though Emily and George are the central figures in Act II, their parents also feature prominently. Dr. and Mrs. Gibbs use the wedding day as an opportunity to reflect on their own marriage, which is portrayed as being quite happy. The Gibbses ponder the complex aspects of love, especially the fears that accompany a wedding and the difficulties of raising a family. The anxieties that await Emily and George are the same ones that awaited Dr. and Mrs. Gibbs years ago. The wedding ceremony itself is not the only ritual passed from generation to generation. Other elements, such as the bride and groom's cold feet and the challenges of handling the practicalities of married life, are just as enduring.

Wilder infuses Act II with a sense of tradition. The Stage Manager's discussion of the specific details of George and Emily's wedding is accompanied by a discussion of the universal ideas surrounding the tradition of marriage. This sense of tradition is emphasized by the sanctity of the choir's music, the formality of the wedding rituals, and the inevitable comparisons drawn between the newlyweds and older married couples. The Stage Manager's comment that only "[o]nce in a thousand times [is marriage] interesting" suggests the generic, traditional quality of the wedding ceremony. Wilder implies that, in general, the significance of an individual marriage lies in its relation to the greater human condition. Indeed, much of the play's action would be unremarkable if taken out of the context of the philosophical and metaphysical ramblings of its characters. Act II illustrates the essence of young love: Wilder does not intend the activities and daily lives of the inhabitants of Grover's Corners to interest us in and of themselves, but rather to encapsulate the nature of life.

ACT III

SUMMARY

*There's something way down deep that's eternal about
every human being.*

(See QUOTATIONS, p. 46)

The stage has been set with three rows of chairs, representing grave-
stones. At the end of the intermission, Mrs. Gibbs, Simon Stimson,
Mrs. Soames, and Wally Webb, among others, take their seats. All
of these characters have died in the intervening years between Act II
and Act III, and the stage has become the local cemetery, situated at
the top of a hill overlooking Grover's Corners. The Stage Manager
appears and announces that another nine years have passed—it is
now the summer of 1913. The Stage Manager talks about the dead,
telling us that the dead lose interest in the living and in earthly mat-
ters. He says that "everybody in their bones knows that something is
eternal," and that the dead spend their time waiting for this eternal
part of their selves to emerge.

A few living people have been hovering at the back of the stage
and now come to the foreground. The Stage Manager introduces
Joe Stoddard, the town's undertaker, who is watching over a freshly
dug grave, and Sam Craig, a cousin of Emily Gibbs. We learn that
Sam left Grover's Corners twelve years ago to go west and has
returned to town for Emily's funeral. Sam reads the headstones, rep-
resented by the characters sitting in chairs. He sees his Aunt Julia,
known to us as Mrs. Gibbs, and Mr. Stimson, who, we learn from
Joe, hanged himself in his attic. Sam asks Joe how Emily died, and
Joe replies that she passed away in childbirth.

A funeral party enters with a casket. Among the mourners are
George, Dr. Gibbs, and the Webbs. While the living characters hud-
dle at the back of the stage, Mrs. Soames and Mrs. Gibbs talk dis-
passionately about the cause of Emily's death. Mrs. Soames
reminisces about George and Emily's wedding. A group standing by
the grave begins singing "Blessed Be the Tie That Binds." Emily
emerges from the funeral party and joins the characters in the cemetery—her body has just been interred. She sits in an empty chair
beside Mrs. Gibbs and tells her mother-in-law all about the
improvements she and George had been making to their farm. Emily
suddenly stops, seemingly struck by an epiphany, and looks at Mrs.

Gibbs. "Live people don't understand," Emily says. Sitting with the dead, now one of them herself, Emily remarks how distant she feels from the living.

Even so, Emily says, she still feels like one of the living, and against the advice of the other dead souls, she decides to go back and relive one happy day from her life. With the assistance of the Stage Manager, Emily goes back to 1899, to the day of her twelfth birthday. It is dawn, and we witness another typical Grover's Corners morning. As Constable Warren, Howie Newsome, and Joe Crowell, Jr. chat in the street outside Emily's house, Mrs. Webb comes downstairs to fix breakfast. Mr. Webb has been away in another town for the last few days, but now he returns home with a surprise gift for his daughter. When Mrs. Webb gives the young Emily her presents, however, the scene becomes unbearable for Emily's deceased soul. Overcome by her observation that human beings go through life without savoring their time on Earth, Emily tells the Stage Manager that she is ready to go back to 1913 and return to the cemetery.

Emily again takes her place next to Mrs. Gibbs. The dead talk and watch the stars come out over Grover's Corners. Emily exclaims that she should have listened to the dead and stayed in her grave. Simon Stimson angrily replies that Emily now understands how the living waste time, trampling on the feelings of others and existing in a self-centered world of "ignorance and blindness." Mrs. Gibbs defends the living, telling Simon that he has not told Emily the whole truth. Still contemplating the stars, one man among the dead recalls his son telling him that starlight takes millions of years to travel to the Earth from its source.

George appears and, overcome with grief, throws himself down in front of Emily's grave, prompting several disapproving comments from the dead souls. As Emily watches her husband lie prostrate on the ground, she asks Mrs. Gibbs, "They don't understand, do they?" The Stage Manager reappears and draws a dark curtain across the stage. He offers a few closing remarks about Grover's Corners as it settles down for the night. Looking at the stars, he says that the Earth may be the only place in the universe where life exists. Winding his watch, he ends the play by telling the audience to go home and get some good rest.

ANALYSIS

Dramatically speaking, very little happens over the course of these three acts, but thematically the play spans the whole of human life, beginning with Dr. Gibbs's delivery of twins, continuing through daily life and a wedding, and concluding with burial and death. The three separate focuses of *Our Town*—"Daily Life," "Love and Marriage," and "Death"—reflect the course of life from its beginning to its middle to its end. Appropriately, the tone of the play changes from act to act. Act I focuses on a rather mundane day in Grover's Corners, and the dialogue is straightforward and informational. In Act II, an increased complexity in the language conveys the heightened state of feeling. Emily and George's conversations, both in high school and on their wedding day, are full of subtleties and periods of awkwardness that demonstrate the couple's deepening emotions. The tone of Act III differs strikingly from that of the earlier scenes. The disinterested dialogue of the dead characters, contrasted with the emotional speeches of live characters in this and other acts, confers a sense of solemnity and inevitability upon death. This last section of the play takes on an almost mystical, religious quality. The Stage Manager's Act I remark that the play will be included in a time capsule to preserve "simple facts" about life suggests that perhaps Emily's death will represent just another recorded event for future generations to study. Emily's experience in Act III, however, shows how the play also delves into emotional response, as she exclaims the flaws and joys of a complex human existence.

The sorrowful, emotional atmosphere of Act III stems not from Emily's death, but from the realization that most people do not cherish life the way they should. Ironically, according to Emily's experience during her flashback, the living despair about the end of life, but do not make much effort to cherish life while they still have it. Emily, however, is only able to realize how precious her life is after she has died. Even the dead characters who insist that Emily should not relive her life do so because it seems they once made the same attempt to return themselves. The dead already have made the painful realization that Emily will soon reach. Wilder reveals to his living audience that most people "don't understand" that the power of life exists not only in the moments of great passion and joy, but in the details of everyday existence as well. When George prostrates himself on Emily's grave at the end of the play, the dead react as if the time for emotion has passed.

SUMMARY & ANALYSIS

The ritualistic quality of the funeral further emphasizes the quality of timelessness and the lack of change that we see in the first two acts. The townspeople view death as a normal facet of life, and though grief-stricken, they follow ceremonial conventions. Joe Stoddard prepares Emily's grave as he has prepared many graves before, and the funeral party sings a hymn just like the many funeral parties before them. Moreover, the song, "Blessed Be the Tie That Binds," appears twice earlier in the play—once during choir practice in Act I, and again during the wedding in Act II. The fact that we hear the song again in this last act underscores the idea that death is just one part of an unchanging human existence.

Even though Wilder focuses on a primarily Christian—and specifically Protestant—town, in the final act he leaves the question of religion up in the air. In Act I, the Stage Manager discusses the multiplicity of churches in the town, emphasizing the idea that faith can take many forms. The choir scene in Act I takes on a decidedly comic tone with the drunken Stimson as choir director, undermining the notion of the church as a sanctuary. We do not see prayers or church services figure heavily in the daily lives of the two families. Even in the Stage Manager's "sermon" in Act II, he refrains from using the word "God" in reference to a higher power. In Act III, though Mrs. Gibbs tells Emily to stay and prepare for "what's ahead" rather than return to the world of the living, Wilder does not clarify where the afterlife will lead.

Instead, Wilder concludes *Our Town* with references to the unfathomable nature of the universe, echoing similar references from earlier in the play. The dead man's remark about the millions of years it takes for starlight to reach the Earth implies that human beings comprise only a small portion of a larger framework. Yet, even so, the Stage Manager says that human life is probably unique and that therefore it has an activity and perhaps a divinity all of its own.

In his opening remarks to Act III, the Stage Manager indicates that the "eternal" lies in each and every human being and in the interactions between human beings. However, the Stage Manager's insistence that most people fail to recognize the eternal in themselves and in those around them during their earthly lives highlights Wilder's contention that though life is transient, it is nonetheless precious. Watching the dead souls, the Stage Manager asks, "Aren't they waitin' for the eternal part in them to come out clear?" His meaning is ambiguous, but it seems that Wilder is indicating that

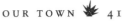

human beings should engage the eternal while on Earth. They do not need to wait until the afterlife in order for their eternal nature to shine forth.

The appearance of Simon Stimson reintroduces the play's socio-political discussion in this final act. With Stimson's comment that people "move about in a cloud of ignorance . . . always at the mercy of one self-centered passion, or another," Wilder yet again gives voice to the social critics who contend that people who blind themselves to the social ills of the world are wasting their time on Earth. Even so, Wilder quiets such relentless criticism through Mrs. Gibbs's rebuttal, putting to rest the notion that life consists only of "ignorance and blindness." Wilder acknowledges that greed and injustice exist in the world, and he does not deny that they probably exist in Grover's Corners too. However, like Mrs. Gibbs, Wilder maintains that much good exists in the world as well.

SUMMARY & ANALYSIS

IMPORTANT QUOTATIONS EXPLAINED

1. So—people a thousand years from now—this is the
    way we were in the provinces north of New York at
    the beginning of the twentieth century.—This is the
    way we were: in our growing up and in our marrying
    and in our living and in our dying.

The Stage Manager makes this declaration in the middle of Act I. He
has just discussed how historical documents tend not to reveal much
about the real lives of ordinary people and has mentioned that he
wants to put a copy of *Our Town* into the time capsule alongside
several more famous texts. The play, he says, will reveal to future
readers facts about human life other than the Treaty of Versailles.
The Stage Manager's position of authority within the play allows
him to speak philosophically and articulate Wilder's own ideas.
This quotation in particular clarifies Wilder's general intent in writing this play. Many dramas, the Stage Manager implies, deal with
moments of heightened emotion or rare events, and many historical
resources relate esoteric incidents. *Our Town*, however, addresses
daily events and traditional, recognizable ceremonies. We witness
through the Gibbs and Webb families the full spectrum of human
existence, from birth to marriage to parenthood to death. The Stage
Manager's direct address to future readers, the "people a thousand
years from now," suggests his wish that *Our Town* persist as a
source of information about the importance of appreciating the sim-
pler details in life.

2.   [P]eople are meant to go through life two by two.
     'Tain't natural to be lonesome.

Mrs. Gibbs makes this remark in Act II, on the morning of George's wedding to Emily, as she comments to her husband on the importance of companionship. Mrs. Gibbs's remark articulates one of the play's central themes: the sanctity of human interactions. This theme is echoed in the repeated singing of the hymn "Blessed Be the Tie that Binds" and in the fact that the narrative structure focuses on the marriage between George and Emily. In context, Mrs. Gibbs's statement pertains to marriage and to the natural tendency for romantic love to flourish between two people. However, her comment also applies in a broader sense to the other, nonromantic relationships that receive attention throughout the play. In fact, Wilder may even privilege platonic companionship and general human connections above romance. Mrs. Gibbs implies that marriage is "natural" and that marriage eradicates loneliness.

In reality, however, some married people remain lonely in the play, like Simon Stimson and his wife. Stimson, the lonely drunk who has "seen a peck of trouble," receives very little active compassion from his fellow townspeople, who never even tell us what his "trouble" is. Without his community's active compassion and care, he becomes even more cynical and pained. Wilder asserts that all loneliness, including loneliness in marriage, is unnatural, and thus implicitly criticizes Mrs. Gibbs's small town idealism. In *Our Town*, Wilder highlights the importance of communication and human connections, literally bringing his audience into contact with his characters by breaking the fourth wall and thereby defying the theatrical convention of separating the actors from the audience.

3. I think that once you've found a person that you're
    very fond of . . . I mean a person who's fond of you,
    too, and likes you enough to be interested in your
    character. . . . Well, I think that's just as important as
    college is, and even more so. That's what I think.

George says these words to Emily while the two sit in Mr. Morgan's drugstore, drinking ice-cream sodas, during the flashback in Act II. This passage is one of the play's crucial moments, when the two young people first reveal their romantic feelings toward one another. George's revelation persuades him to forego agriculture school and stay in Grover's Corners with Emily instead. Rather than set love aside in order to continue his education, George prefers to focus on what he considers truly important. By prioritizing love above college, George illustrates the human desire for companionship that pervades the play. As the Stage Manager says a little later, our millions of ancestors "set out to live two-by-two also." *Our Town* is a play about community as much as it is about individual experience. George and Emily simply exhibit the desire for love that all human beings share. This moment also suggests that college may not be a natural or inevitable stage of human development. Love, however, is natural—at least in the context of Wilder's view of life as a general movement from birth to death.

QUOTATIONS

4. We all know that something is eternal. And it ain't houses and it ain't names, and it ain't earth, and it ain't even the stars . . . everybody knows in their bones that something is eternal, and that something has to do with human beings. All the greatest people ever lived have been telling us that for five thousand years and yet you'd be surprised how people are always losing hold of it. There's something way down deep that's eternal about every human being.

The Stage Manager delivers this passage during his long monologue at the beginning of Act III. This quotation prefaces the opinions of the dead, who believe that human beings "don't understand" the true significance of existence. While living, they say, human beings tend to get so caught up in day-to-day details and responsibilities, feeling so obligated to the mundane chores of daily life that they often miss the meaningful nature of human existence. The Stage Manager echoes this sentiment here, implying that human beings possess the gut knowledge that something is eternal but lack an understanding of what constitutes the eternal. Like the dead in Act III, the Stage Manager insists that the "eternal" exists within each and every human being, and that people can share this eternal nature through their daily interactions with one another.

The Stage Manager's words thus highlight Wilder's interest in finding the eternal among the details of daily life. Humans possess individual eternal souls that may live on after physical death, but their interactions with one another while still on Earth may exceed even the unfathomable beauty of the afterlife. The Stage Manager considers what the souls in the play are "waitin' for," but he can only pose his thoughts in the form of a question: "Aren't they waitin' for the eternal part in them to come out clear?" Wilder depicts the dead souls in Act III primarily in order to acknowledge the transience of human life on Earth. This transience gives life its beauty and its eternal, divine value, regardless of whatever unknown events may lie ahead. *Our Town*, though ending with the afterlife, insists that the eternal exists on Earth during each and every moment of human interaction.

5. Do any human beings ever realize life while they live it?—every, every minute?

Emily asks this question of the Stage Manager at the end of Act III, after she has revisited her twelfth birthday. The Stage Manager answers that humans indeed do not realize life, except for perhaps the "saints and poets, maybe." Perhaps the play's best-known passage, these words emphasize the value of everyday events. Throughout the play, the characters place importance on moments of ceremony and consequence, such as George and Emily's wedding and Emily's funeral. But the characters do not seem to value or make an emotional connection to the daily activities of their rather ordinary lives.

Instead of attempting to "realize life" at every moment, the inhabitants of Grover's Corners—and people the world over, by implication—often lack any sense of wonder at what passes before their eyes every day. When Emily relives her twelfth birthday, she futilely tries to get her mother really to look at her and not take her presence for granted. This experience causes Emily to realize that during her own life, she herself did not pay enough attention to detail and did not appreciate her family and her town the way she does now that she is dead. Emily's remark directly precedes her return to the cemetery, and it signals her resignation to the realm of the dead souls. Emily is pained by her recognition that human beings waste great opportunities at every moment, and her realization dampens her desire to return to the world of the living.

KEY FACTS

FULL TITLE
Our Town

AUTHOR
Thornton Wilder

TYPE OF WORK
Play

GENRE
Wilder's play defies most conventional theatrical genres. It is neither a comedy nor a tragedy, neither a romance nor a farce. It is, rather, a contemplative work concerning the human experience.

LANGUAGE
English

TIME AND PLACE WRITTEN
1934–1938, United States

DATE OF FIRST PUBLICATION
1938

PUBLISHER
Coward-McCann, Inc.

NARRATOR
The play does not contain the sort of narrator that a novel might, but the Stage Manager does act as a narrator figure, guiding us through the action.

TONE
The Stage Manager, essentially the play's narrator, often speaks directly to the audience in an authoritative and informative voice. He is polite but firm in his cues to other characters. However, he also appears quite contemplative at times, especially during his longer monologues. Many characters in the play also have moments of philosophical reverie, and the play's dialogue and exposition tends to be nostalgic and introspective.

SETTING (TIME)

Act I takes place on May 7, 1901; Act II takes place on July 7, 1904, with a flashback to approximately one year earlier; Act III takes place in the summer of 1913, with a flashback to February 11, 1899

SETTING (PLACE)

Grover's Corners, New Hampshire

PROTAGONISTS

The most significant figure in the play is the Stage Manager, who orchestrates the action onstage and serves as the glue that holds disparate scenes together. However, the narrative action revolves around Emily Webb and George Gibbs, who fall in love and get married.

MAJOR CONFLICT

Humans constantly struggle to realize that the eternal exists even within ordinary events.

RISING ACTION

The depiction of daily life; the first romantic conversation between George and Emily; the couple's wedding

CLIMAX

After dying in childbirth and joining the dead souls in the cemetery, Emily returns to relive a day from her earthly life, which makes her realize how little the living appreciate the value of life.

FALLING ACTION

Emily returns to the world of the dead souls in the cemetery.

THEMES

The transience of human life; the importance of companionship; the artificiality of the theater

MOTIFS

The stages of life; natural cycles; morning; the manipulation of time

SYMBOLS

The time capsule; Howie Newsome and the Crowell boys; the hymn "Blessed Be the Tie That Binds"

KEY FACTS

FORESHADOWING

George and Emily's sweet conversations in Act I point toward a burgeoning romance in Act II. The Stage Manager's indications in Act I that this play will discuss marriage and then death clue us in to the direction that George and Emily's relationship, which is at the center of the play, will take.

KEY FACTS

STUDY QUESTIONS & ESSAY TOPICS

STUDY QUESTIONS

1.   *How does the temporal structure of* Our Town *reflect and influence the main ideas of the play?*

Our Town does not simply depict ordinary life in a small town, but engages deeper subject matter such as the influence of time on human lives. Future readers of the play, according to the Stage Manager, will be able to discern from the play's content the ways in which ordinary humans' lives move and change "in our growing up and in our marrying and in our living and in our dying." The three-act structure of the play reflects this focus by mirroring the stages of a human life: Act I begins with a birth in early morning and offers a glimpse of daily life in Grover's Corners; Act II shows us courtship and an afternoon wedding; Act III culminates with death and the afterlife, and as the play ends, night has fallen. Although scenes of the evening do exist in other parts of the play, the play's overarching structure begins with dawn and ends with dusk. Significantly, however, Wilder juxtaposes the momentum of individual lives with the unchanging nature of human existence. The play returns again and again to scenes that take place in the morning—the milkman delivering milk, the paperboy delivering the paper—indicating a timelessness and lack of change despite the passage of years. With a structural emphasis on stability, a single marriage becomes representative of many marriages, past, present, and future, and a single romance becomes representative of universal feelings of love.

2. *As little happens in the play in terms of dramatic events,
the thematic content of the play and Wilder's attempt to
engage his audience actively take center stage. The success
of the play depends on its ability to break down the so-
called "fourth wall" between the audience and the actors.
How does Wilder break down this barrier between the
audience and the action onstage?*

Throughout the play, Wilder turns theatrical conventions inside
out, exposing the seams of his drama. A particularly vivid example
of the liberty that Wilder takes with dramatic conventions is his
breaking down of the fourth wall in Act I. Here, Mr. Webb takes
questions from members of the audience, who are actually characters in the play seated in the audience. By interspersing his characters among his audience, Wilder groups them all into the same
reality. Wilder also emphasizes the artifice of his play by allowing
the audience to see how the sets change and by having the Stage
Manager announce when it is time for intermission.

The Stage Manager, whose title suggests that he should be a
member of the crew rather than the cast, embodies Wilder's attempt
to break the fourth wall. The Stage Manager exists both in the
world of the audience and the world of the play, sometimes interrupting the action to provide information, and sometimes assuming
various roles within the play. By conversing directly with the audience, the Stage Manager requires the audience to participate in the
theatrical experience rather than simply observe a slice of small
town life. The play's title breaks down the barrier as well: Grover's
Corners is not literally our town, but we realize that metaphorically,
it could be.

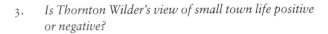

3.   *Is Thornton Wilder's view of small town life positive
     or negative?*

Wilder wrote *Our Town* in the 1930s, a time of widespread economic hardship that led many to expect authors to use their works
as instruments of social criticism. Wilder's story of small town life
exists within a genre that often found authors attempting to reveal
the corruption beneath the surface of the seeming tranquility of
rural life. On one hand, *Our Town* seems to offer a defiant, over-
whelmingly positive portrayal of a fictional New England town
around 1900. The children appear well behaved, the parents appear
decent and hardworking, and all one must do to find love is ask a
neighbor to have an ice-cream soda.

On the other hand, however, Wilder does not idealize the town
of Grover's Corners. He actively encourages us to think about the
aforementioned criticism of small town life by actually voicing such
criticism within the play, during the question-and-answer section
with Mr. Webb. Moreover, the way the characters relate to Simon
Stimson reveals much about the limitations of small town life. They
talk about Simon's alcoholism and refer opaquely to his "peck of
trouble," but they never clarify what constitutes Simon's trouble or
make a concerted effort to help him. Instead, people like Dr. Gibbs
allow Simon to wallow in his loneliness, saying that he just is not
made for small town life. Ultimately, Wilder never answers the
question of who holds responsibility for such troubles. However,
whether or not one condemns the residents of Grover's Corners for
not paying attention to certain troubles seems irrelevant to the
major themes of Wilder's play. Although problems and hypocrisy
exist everywhere, Wilder still finds humanity and power in the sim-
plicity of this small town.

SUGGESTED ESSAY TOPICS

1.   Discuss the character of the Stage Manager. How does he fit into the world of the play?

2.   Analyze the play's portrayal of love, courtship, and married life. How do these aspects of life operate within the play's overarching themes?

3.   Why is Emily unhappy when she tries to relive part of her life after she dies? Defend your answer.

4.   Discuss the conception of the "eternal" in the play. What does the Stage Manager believe "eternal" means? Do the events of the play agree with him? Why or why not?

Review & Resources

Quiz

1. Where is *Our Town* set?

   A. Spoon River, Illinois
   B. Grover's Corners, New Hampshire
   C. Amity Harbor, Washington
   D. Winesburg, Ohio

2. In what year does the play begin?

   A. 1860
   B. 1950
   C. 1913
   D. 1901

3. What does the play's set look like at the beginning of the play?

   A. The stage is bare except for two benches
   B. The stage is bare except for two tables, some chairs, a bench, and two trellises
   C. The stage is set up to look like Main Street
   D. The stage has two houses painted on the back wall, one for the Webbs and one for the Gibbses

4. As the play begins, where has Dr. Gibbs been?

   A. Spending the night with his mistress in a motel room
   B. Delivering twin babies
   C. Visiting a dying woman
   D. At a medical convention in Manchester

5. What does Mr. Webb do for a living?

   A. He is a selectman
   B. He is the editor of the local newspaper
   C. He is a duck hunter
   D. He is a surgeon

6. Where does Mrs. Gibbs want to take a vacation?

    A. Florida
    B. Rome
    C. New York City
    D. Paris

7. Which characters does the Stage Manager bring out to tell the audience about the town?

    A. Professor Willard and Mr. Webb
    B. Professor Willard and Mrs. Gibbs
    C. George Gibbs and Mrs. Soames
    D. Dr. Gibbs and Constable Warren

8. Who is the Lady in the Box?

    A. The Stage Manager's lovely assistant
    B. A prisoner in the local jail
    C. George's pet name for Emily when she sits by her window
    D. An actress placed in the audience

9. Which of the following does not get deposited in the time capsule?

    A. A copy of *Our Town*
    B. A copy of the Bible
    C. A picture of the Stage Manager
    D. An issue of *The Sentinel*

10. What does George want to do after high school?

    A. Study at Harvard
    B. Take over his uncle's farm
    C. Become a doctor
    D. Become a teacher

11. From what affliction does the choirmaster suffer?

    A. Alcoholism
    B. Cancer
    C. Insomnia
    D. Grief over his father's death

12. What is the name of the song the choir sings several times during the play?

    A.   "Blessed Be the Tie That Binds"
    B.   "Happy Birthday"
    C.   "The Hallelujah Chorus"
    D.   "The Wedding March"

13. What is the weather like at the beginning of Act II?

    A.   It is snowing
    B.   It is raining
    C.   It is sunny
    D.   It is foggy

14. Who gets married in Act II?

    A.   George and Rebecca
    B.   Wally and Rebecca
    C.   George and Emily
    D.   Mr. Webb and Mrs. Gibbs

15. What sport does George play in high school?

    A.   Soccer
    B.   Football
    C.   Baseball
    D.   Basketball

16. During the flashback in Act II, where does George take Emily after she accuses him of being stuck up?

    A.   Home to meet his parents
    B.   To the field to watch him play baseball
    C.   To get an ice-cream soda
    D.   To eat dinner at a restaurant

17. Who gets nervous before the wedding?

    A.   Both George and Emily
    B.   Only George
    C.   Only Emily
    D.   George and Emily's parents

REVIEW & RESOURCES

18. Who acts as the minister at the wedding?

    A. The Stage Manager
    B. Constable Warren
    C. The Mayor
    D. Dr. Gibbs

19. What is Sam Craig's relationship to Emily?

    A. He is her ex-boyfriend
    B. He is her cousin
    C. He is an old friend from school
    D. He is one of her high school teachers

20. What is the cause of Emily's death?

    A. Old age
    B. Cancer
    C. A car accident
    D. Complications during childbirth

21. What day from her earthly life does Emily decide to revisit?

    A. Her wedding day
    B. The day of her first child's birth
    C. Her twelfth birthday
    D. Her high school graduation

22. What happens when Emily goes back and relives the past?

    A. She is unable to bear it and returns to the cemetery
    B. She decides to remain there
    C. She realizes how boring life is
    D. She finds everything has changed

23. Who leads Emily back to the cemetery?

    A. Mrs. Gibbs
    B. The Stage Manager
    C. Mr. Webb
    D. An angel

24. Who comes and lays prostrate beside Emily's grave at the end of the play?

    A. Mr. Webb
    B. Mrs. Webb
    C. The Stage Manager
    D. George

25. What is the Stage Manager's final action?

    A. He bows to the audience
    B. He winds his watch
    C. He waves good-bye to the audience
    D. He draws the curtain across the stage

SUGGESTIONS FOR FURTHER READING

BLANK, MARTIN, ED. *Critical Essays on Thornton Wilder.* New York: G.K. Hall, 1996.

BLANK, MARTIN, DALMA HUNYADI BRUNAUER, AND DAVID GARRETT IZZO, EDS. *Thornton Wilder: New Essays.* West Cornwall, Connecticut: Locust Hill Press, 1999.

BURBANK, REX J. *Thornton Wilder.* Boston: Twayne Publishers, 1978.

CASTRONOVO, DAVID. *Thornton Wilder.* New York: Ungar, 1986.

DE KOSTER, KATIE, ED. *Readings on Thornton Wilder.* San Diego: Greenhaven Press, 1998.

HABERMAN, DONALD C. *Our Town: An American Play.* Boston: Twayne Publishers, 1989.

LIFTON, PAUL. *Vast Encyclopedia: The Theatre of Thornton Wilder.* Westport, Connecticut: Greenwood Press, 1995.

WALSH, MARY ELLEN WILLIAMS. *A Vast Landscape: Time in the Novels of Thornton Wilder.* Pocatello, Idaho: Idaho State University Press, 1979.

WILDER, AMOS N. *Thornton Wilder and His Public.* Cleveland: W. Collins Publishers, 1980.

REVIEW & RESOURCES

A Note on the Type

The typeface used in SparkNotes study guides is Sabon, created by master typographer Jan Tschichold in 1964. Tschichold revolutionized the field of graphic design twice: first with his use of asymmetrical layouts and sanserif type in the 1930s when he was affiliated with the Bauhaus, then by abandoning assymetry and calling for a return to the classic ideals of design. Sabon, his only extant typeface, is emblematic of his latter program: Tschichold's design is a recreation of the types made by Claude Garamond, the great French typographer of the Renaissance, and his contemporary Robert Granjon. Fittingly, it is named for Garamond's apprentice, Jacques Sabon.

SPARKNOTES
TEST PREPARATION
GUIDES

The SparkNotes team figured it was time to cut standardized tests down to size. We've studied the tests for you, so that SparkNotes test prep guides are:

Smarter:
Packed with critical-thinking skills and test-
taking strategies that will improve your score.

Better:
Fully up to date, covering all new features of the tests,
with study tips on every type of question.

Faster:
Our books cover exactly what you need to
know for the test. No more, no less.

SparkNotes Study Guides: